Sledding the Valley of the Shadow

Laura Foley

Fernwood
PRESS

Sledding the Valley of the Shadow
©2024 by Laura Foley

Fernwood Press
Newberg, Oregon
www.fernwoodpress.com

Printed in the United States of America

Cover and page design: Mareesa Fawver Moss
Cover art: "Joy" by Clara Giménez
Author photo: Clara Giménez

ISBN 978-1-59498-149-4

Also by Laura Foley

Ice Cream for Lunch: A Grandparents Handbook (forthcoming in 2025)
It's This
Everything We Need: Poems from El Camino (chapbook)
Why I Never Finished My Dissertation
WTF (chapbook)
Night Ringing
Joy Street (chapbook)
The Glass Tree
Syringa
Mapping the Fourth Dimension

In *Sledding the Valley of the Shadow*, Laura Foley tells the tale of how we suffer, how we are delighted, how we may triumph, and we find ourselves "immersed like otters, in the buoyancy of life on Earth, in time taking us and re-making us." Joy emerges in these poems even while Foley contemplates "another brush with the great beyond ... keening,/ just outside the screen" and the reader finds herself "recalled ... time and time again." Like the speaker in "The Beauty of the Beast," we are reminded to "dare, in early heat, the scariest,/most gorgeous beach (we) know," to immerse ourselves in that "sweet coolness." These are poems of transformation and transcendence, trouble and redemption, distress and comfort where "the dark underside of the bridge becomes a riverine cathedral"—and we join the speaker "soothed by its cool shadows, floating at ease."

—CAROL POTTER
author of *What Happens Next is Anyone's Guess*

The path of Laura Foley's remarkable new poetry collection begins with a "huge, black-winged bat ... this shadow of death" circling her; then the shadow fades into background as we learn more about Laura's history, people she cares about, and her delight in walking on pathways in Vermont and Spain. She is a keen observer with a gift for creating concise, zen-like descriptions—not just visual but rich in all the senses. Just as I was settling into the poetry and feeling connected to the poet, the shadow tried a return—in harrowing health crises for Laura and her wife, Clara, followed by the Covid pandemic. Amazingly though, the book doesn't descend into pathos but rather is full of joy, humor, and, most of all, love; as in "The Ineffable," describing Clara's healing.... "Back in the house, she practices vibrato,/ her deep alto rising through the floor boards,/ the roof on the house rising too,/ the sky opening for both of us." Yes, this is a collection of strong poems, but it is also a really compelling, redemptive story.

—KALI LIGHTFOOT,
author of *Pelted by Flowers*

This collection is a striking meditation on "love made visible." Its poems nudge us to pay careful attention to what's happening within and beyond us. They invite us to greater intimacy with our lives even while smacking up against the hard stuff of living.

—PHYLLIS COLE-DAI,
co-editor of *Poetry of Presence* anthologies

For Clara, my love

Contents

I.

Not a Metaphor

Not the phone's jarring interruption
in this moment of wonder—

not Dad's late night news
of our sudden loss of my teenage sister, Alix,

not this huge, black-winged bat circling us
as I clutch our newborn daughter, I birthed at home.

Not a simile, this child with traces of blood
on her arms—nor these stained sheets

I rose from moments ago in hope
of sharing joy so pure I couldn't feel my feet.

Not this bat flapping so close
to the seat of my rational sense, this shadow

of death that makes me duck, as I hold
my baby, still nameless, to my chest.

Our Own Orion

No need to travel to Iceland for northern lights,
to cruise rough seas for glimpses of a different sky,
we just crack the door, and peer over banks
of thigh-deep snow, to taste our own
frosted slice of night. No need for red and green
streaks or solar flares, or even a lunar eclipse,
just our own Orion with his hunter's bow,
bright stars in a moonless time, whose greater darkness
further defines his more distant place
in endless space and time, we claim by naming.

Someone

I once lived on a great wide river,
a time of deep aloneness, after loss.
How soothing it was to watch waters passing,
sunlight reflected in circular currents,
a white moon cresting
above the shadowed mountain.
I miss the river, though not
the hushed quietness of that time,
the endless plumbing of depths
I never guessed, which nonetheless
led me to choose—a wife
calling me from another room,
as she is now, to come downstairs for tea,
steeped to the color of the river.

The Once Invisible Garden

How did I come to be
this particular version of me,
and not some other, this morning
of purple delphiniums
blooming like royalty,
destined to meet these three dogs
asleep at my feet, and not others—
this soft summer morning,
sitting on her screened porch
become ours, our wind chime
singing of wind and time,
yellow-white digitalis
feeding bees and filling me—
and more abundance to come:
basil, tomatoes, zucchini.
What luck or fate, instinct,
or grace brought me here—
in shade, beneath hidden stars,
a soft, summer morning,
seeing with my whole being,
love made visible.

The River

We each that summer didn't just dip in like wing tips skimming
the surface, but more than birds, more than Pegasus—we
immersed like otters, in the buoyancy of life on Earth, in time
taking us and remaking us, in waves lapping over us, its liquid
propulsion and flow—showing how we are the particles of us, of
our bodies, my children and me needing healing, after the loss
of father and husband—our bodies allowing the river—pushing
and wading, our thighs working overtime, to where the old
covered bridge shadowed the depths we floated over, as surface
water lapped us, staring at the dark underside of the bridge that
preceded all of us and would certainly continue after—arcing over
us like a riverine cathedral—soothed by its cool shadows, floating
at ease before rejoining the current—wind racing wavelets over
us, so we bobbed like boats in choppy waters, till our legs finally
lifted us from the shallow edges, escaping the sweeping-away to
some beckoning sea—we'd leave the river for solid ground, until
heat or grief recalled us, time and time again.

The Frother Whisk

When I discover, one dark morning,
a year after our nation's calamity,
my latte maker's missing
its most important part—
an inner screw that, normally,
holds the frother whisk in place,
allowing the foam to coalesce
to serve a greater purpose—
I call the urgent Nespresso line,
whose representative reassures,
as I wish our leader could—
they understand the crisis,
will hurry a replacement
to our hilltop in Vermont,
and what else can they do
to help? *Please whisk yourselves
into the Oval Office.*
Replace the lost-screw in-chief—
overnight service preferred.

Intimations of Adulthood

The whole long drive south,
she keeps Kari's salamander safe,
in a box on her lap, feeding it leaves,
per Kari's instructions.
When she plays the alphabet game
with her mom, she keeps one eye
on her best friend's lizard. On arrival,
the balmy wind on her legs, skinny
and pale from winter, eases some tension.
She steps into woods near the motel,
frees the reptilian city dweller,
who spreads its jaws wide,
traps a fat, juicy fly in one gulp,
disappears into the tropical night—
leaving her alone in the black gulf
of horrified silence
she learns will always follow violence.

We Are Ready

No more silence as we are being forced—
no more hiding, no waiting
for drunken boys to leave the room
so we can sneak egress,

no more young men pinballing down stairs,
careening to Ivy Leagues and good careers,
leaving broken girls in their wakes.

We, with our messiness, are ready to mess with them,
with our menstruation, procreation, and breast milk dripping;
we are filling Senate seats and floors,
we are breaching the hallowed doors of power.

Let the aging, suited men turn red.
Let them shout, rant, and cry on live TV.
They've taken their playlist from a president
who teaches how to hate,

but we, who bear and birth the fruits of love,
destined by biology to caretake, and not forsake
compassion—are breaking our silence to educate—
a senator today, in an elevator, on the state of our nation.

Conjuration

Wearing deep-cleated snow shoes,
    I climb the hill behind our house,

kept company by my loyal canines.
    We admire the summit view, familiar peaks

made new by clouds of fresh snow,
    then begin the long descent,

not steeply down, but through
    the neighbor's welcoming snow fields,

past shadowed pines, leafless maples,
    oaks that hold their leaves like aces.

Alys waits for me, but Chloe runs off,
    returns when called, then doesn't.

Alys and I trudge for miles as I call,
    through empty fields and see:

no deer, no dog, not even a squirrel
    for comfort, as the blizzard wind begins.

I nearly lose myself on a steep cliff—
    slipping down through icy woods,

cleats clattering like a trolley off its rails.
    At the bottom, still far from home,

I brush myself off,
    hearing the storm's discord within,

my angry monologue at the dog—
    then a purer note directing me:

Dear Spirit, I plead,
  gesturing up through empty trees—

May she come safely home.
  I conjure an image of her thick, healthy body,

loving face and then, at the next turn,
  she bounds round the corner toward me.

East of Eden

Driving out of Iowa,
summer sun behind us
angry and red,
slanting into the eyes
of a westbound trucker.
A buck bounds out,
shining muscles and ribs—
struck by the unswerving
eighteen-wheeler.
We glimpse
the animal's torso, back legs,
front, head and antlers
suspended, each
glistening pink from sun.
My young daughter,
wary of her emotions,
aware she rarely fits
social expectations,
blurts out that death
is kind of thrilling—
and though a wiser part of me
agrees, I insist on outward grieving
and compassionate prayers,
as together
we barrel east.

The Dive

She arrives in New York, from Ireland, at twenty-one,
marries a man who will, for sport, dive into the Hudson,
but one time misses, hitting the dock edge,

which is why, widowed, with two children,
daughter weak from polio, Mrs. D. becomes my nanny,
my home at home, till I'm grown.

Decades later, I still see sun burnishing silver
the deadly river's surface, as he takes the fateful leap
that will bring her to me.

The Something

Time to notice drops of dew
on every fallen leaf, to draw a finger
through the tiny pools of light,

to watch a body's shadow
casting backward on the leaves,
to feel the sun's surprising heat,

this late October day.
Time to feel the veil of—something—
the *something* that exists

between me and her, invisibly pulling,
as I sit in sunlight waiting
for a single leaf to drop,

and catch it mid-flight.
I can *feel* her texting—*please bring mushrooms,
I want to make a soup for you.*

Daddy and the Beast

Last night I dreamt the president
stalked me in my kitchen.

Last night I dreamt the self-proclaimed
pussy-grabbing president married my mother.

I dreamed the leader of the free world chanted
Lock her up, at me, from my kitchen sink.

I dreamed of trying to please, and giving up trying to please,
a raging beast. I gave up springing from my activities

to greet him at the door, gave up always giving more,
shouting, *My father is dead, you are not my father,*

and, *Not every woman adores a fascist.*
Last night I dreamt my father, the doctor,

was not this bully, though he bullied me,
as he worked to heal strangers—

and the stranger he became,
my father locked up in war by the Japanese,

a difficult father I learned to love,
dead now, to me and everyone, *Dead, Mr. President,*

I dreamt I said, as I descended winding stairs,
pulling my sweatshirt hood around my ears,

but still hearing our common end, *dead, dead,*
drumming the quotidian rhythm in my head.

Letter to Sally

You liked my solitude, devotion to poetry and meditation.
We had done the hard work of raising children,
you five boys, me two boys and a girl.
All were grown, we could focus, without guilt, on our art.

You made a painting-collage, a gift you said reminded you
of me, a laughing Nepalese woman with headdress,
short hiking skirt. How complimented I felt,
how seen, now I wonder if you saw the you in me.

Your relationship to the land was an industry,
your garden a canvas worked tirelessly
to bring forth life, alchemized to tinctures, jams,
teas, and sauces, your pantry turned edible art gallery.

Yet, when COPD made it hard for you to breathe,
you refused the peace-destroying oxygen machine,
and, worn by shingles pain, you planned
to stop eating, after you put the garden to bed,

after visits from your children, their spouses,
your grandchild, after a gathering of women friends.
We met by the pond, told stories, read poems,
sang, and burned notebooks, letters, in a ritual fire.

Some of us cried. Your dog circled us running,
swam in the pond, unbothered by its murky depths.
You asked me, as chaplain, to sprinkle its water
with a wand-branch on all of us, a bookend baptism.

Though your lifelong slenderness had turned emphatic,
you showed no lack of energy,
practically dancing up and down the path,
determined to leave the planet at the apex of illness—

hoping your resolve to go with grace would hold.
When I received word, one soft October morning,
before frost or snow, I could only breathe thanks
for leaving us so much of your soul.

Our Rescue

Clara and I, hiking
on the edge of a glacial lake,
fall suddenly, plunging
through a tunnel
of blue-white light, as I shout
my love for her—
the right last words
for the end of our lives.
When we awake, in hospital,
the trauma nurse explains
a glacier calved,
tumbling us into icy water,
helicopters, divers
coordinated our rescue,
detailed in newspapers,
I can't wait to read—
as soon as I wake from the dream.

Mackerel

Sally's busy, she writes, in her last email to us,
sloughing away her mortal coil,
has almost stopped noticing
fleeting thoughts
of a mackerel sandwich.

I find myself, in the days
after her death, caught like a fish
in a net of wondering: mackerel
salad or grilled on panini,
smoked, fried, or paired with avocado?

Something I've never tried,
but might now, smacked
like a mackerel onto the deck
of the unknowable.

II.

In the Village Store

As a woman and I wait
in a snaking line to pay,
a man cuts in front,
and she catches him, insists he retreat,
but he, angry, I assume,
from last week's election,
the president's drubbing,
snarls: *You're one of the damn Dems*,
and *Not a lady*, assuming, I presume,
that she wants to embody
such an antiquated state,
while my nose twitches like a rabbit
caught napping in a coyote den,
wondering if I must choose
a side to leap to, as a chasm opens
between the chocolate aisle and the cheese,
as she points her finger like a light saber—
screeching, *his butt is as big as Trump's*,
fat, I might judge,
from his eating too much beef,
as she displays her blue-jeaned posterior,
like a peacock's tail, firm and toned,
I assume, as she pats it,
from dieting and yoga,
here in Vermont,
where he likely presumes
we all vote for Bernie the Socialist—
New Age heathens in want of evangelical saving,
while we profess enlightenment,
but sometimes act like orangutans,
squabbling over bananas
in the wilds of Borneo.

Madre

As the train rumbles side to side,
as we leave the town of Clara's birth,
we move into the hot, dry plain,
green after recent, sweet spring rains—
remembering how we sat
in her mother's flat, abode of fifty years,

as thunder sang its omen tones,
as clouds—dark grey against still-blue sky—
let go their heavy load on us,
on the city, on all of Spain—
and how today the sky's all sun,
swept clean after last night's weeping.

This morning we crossed
the not-yet busy street, as her mother
leaned over the balcony,
her small frame bent with age,
her spine *un perro rabioso que muerde*—
a rabid dog she can't bite back—

we and she called and waved,
as we turned the sunny corner,
our backpacks the last she sees
as she turns away,
closing the casement window,
to sit alone and think of us.

Postmortem Parenting

I.

She comes to me in the dental chair—
or I go into her, mouth propped open,
while others strap a rubber dam over it—

Mom's breathing choked, by a bite of steak
caught in her throat, dying alone on the floor—
willing myself back from panic, I note their names,

Angel, the assistant, and Angela, dentist—
guarded as Mom wasn't, by wings and light,
their gentleness of touch, professional skill,

quickly cutting a breathing hole
in smothering rubber,
so I don't struggle like she did, to breathe.

I refuse anesthetic, focus on my breath,
easing smoothly in—breath flowing calmly out—
relax my outstretched legs and arms,

body breathing through every pore,
palms open to receive the moment,
grating drill fading, as Mom hovers,

and fades further into memory—
my banging on her bedroom door,
barricaded against Dad's rage—

but she pulls it open for me.
We play house on her bed,
walled by pillows, roofed by sheets,

creating a temporary sanctuary,
where we both breathe
a little easier,

in the new home we've made,
the home I find again, today,
in the dental chair.

II.

In the dental chair, my heart banging
against my ribs like a prisoner
in a burning jail, I remember
how cold Dad was, in cashmere coat,
well-shined leather shoes, shivering
as we walked from East End to York,
each step he took, among his last on Earth.

I imagine gravity dragging at his weight,
the heavy slowness of his gait.
If each of us cannot be anywhere
other than where we are, please explain
how I connect with the dead like this,
whenever the dental dam goes in,
whenever they say to me, *be still.*

III.

To my surprise this time, they both hover
by the dental chair, where I ache
with a broken molar.

I may have prayed for them, a little,
in a vague, unbelieving way—
who better to call on in pain,

than those who remember
when the tooth was new?
My parents, divorced

when I was nine,
now long deceased,
unite by my side.

In case I'm too obtuse,
Stand By Me wafts in,
over the radio.

Coastal Globe

We walked by gulls gathering for the night,
as seals rose from the sea, looking curiously
at us, before curling under icy black water.
A herd of porpoise emerged, dark fins
churning waves. In a chaos of sound, gulls
lifted from the cliff, filled the pink sky around us,
scavenging the porpoises' feeding frenzy.
Sky purpled, sea turned placid blue as the sun set,
as we walked home, arm in arm in the dark,
under the sudden globe of stars, as if some great hand
planned to shake us up.

The Beauty of the Beast

I dare, in early heat, the scariest,
most gorgeous beach I know,
where, in recent times,
one young man
was pulled to his watery grave
by a post-storm wave, another
lost a leg to a Great White,
mistaking him for a seal. I see one
this morning—not a shark, but
shark's breakfast. Still,
seeking a moment's buoyancy,
immersion in sweet coolness,
I jump in, paddle about,
and, as I step out, am struck—
not by a shark, but a stone,
wave-hurled full force
at my skin; and so, hobbling, bleeding,
I retreat from the beach
to sip coffee on the porch,
contemplating another brush
with the Great Beyond
I can still hear, keening,
just outside the screen.

Still Savoring

I savored the anticipation
of an intimate evening
at home with my beloved—
our favorite program,
and, after dinner,
a sandwich of chocolates,
rich milk and sweet bitter,
capping the soft summer day.
I had climbed the steep hill—
green valley stretched wide,
swum in the neighbor's pond,
cool and delicious on my skin.
I had begun to slice a ripe avocado,
sliding the knife
through creamy goodness, then
leaned my head against the chair—
my heart racing
two hundred beats a minute,
ambulance on its way—EMTs very busy,
very serious, on our front lawn,
lifting me in, red lights flashing,
injecting my veins as the sun's
deep pinks bled into the night
I could still savor
through outstretched feet.

Bumpy Country

As the medics lift my stretcher into air,
and wriggle it into the ambulance,
as if it might not fit,
I mouth, *I hope they don't drop me*, to my wife,
who stands on the ground below,
and I find myself wondering,
as I'm sped to the hospital,
as my heart does its too-quick samba rhythm,
as if to dance me to the edge of time,
as the IV bag bangs back and forth,
as we travel bumpy country,
if those words to Clara were my last, and if so,
whether it's best, to end with a laugh.

Offstage

Alone, deep in the hemlock woods,
I lean on an old stone wall, alive to its grit,

near a large dislodged rock—perhaps extracted
by the bear I saw yesterday,

wondering how far, or near,
the beast might have rambled.

I listen to pileated woodpecker's
rat-a-tat-tat, a distant saw's high whine,

a mower's rumble from the low valley,
and hear The Bard's savage clamor,

his *Well may I get aboard—*
I never saw the heavens so dim by day,

as I re-see the *ursus Americanus,*
like a character in a play, or my potential fetch—

Exit, pursued by a bear
hidden in the wings,

as shaded ash leaves undulate
in the breezeless air.

What Seems Today

falling in darkness   in cold dark water

regaining consciousness   on the shore   of nowhere I know

on railroad tracks   to somewhere

almost familiar   shall I fly again   over the cold dark deep

that calls to me   like the keening   of a beloved

shall I descend   to unconscious depths of sea

knowing corn husk angels   will save me   understanding

without speech   it isn't time   to travel   past the ambulance

not time to not see   the earthly lights

swirling red and blue warning   hoping

to bring someone back   from the edge   lights

that say bend your head in prayer   for one who needs care

not that final welcoming light   that will one day come

but not   it seems   today

When My Uncle Dies at Ninety

My children and I text his pride
in being left-handed, his mug
that spilled water on us
as he chuckled,
if you drank it right-handed;
love for his composter evident
in the care he took
teaching us to spin its lever;
the squirrely nature of his collecting:
books, stamps, world flags,
antique Mason jars;
his compassion in trapping
a woodchuck to set free
a few miles down the road.
In five texts, we arrive
at the measure of a man.

Sacred Web

When I give a sliver of my atria
to the surgeon's knife,
which will enter, through a probe,
the chambers of my heart,
to weld and cauterize—
will he find my veins a beautiful filigree,
the electrical workings of an intricate machine,
the many loves I've owned,
the soul playing host?
Will I sense, in the half-light
of unconsciousness,
from anesthesia's bardo,
his illumination?
Will I derive comfort from his name,
Sangha, spiritual community,
from the cleanliness of his hands,
from his speech,
whose bell tones seem to chime:
You and I will be fine,
in this sacred web of three:
you, me, and divinity.

On Earth

I find myself, this cloudy spring day,
on a quiet country road,
wild geese nesting in cow fields
on one hand, idle blackbirds
singing in wetlands, on the other,
streams trickling free of ice,
beavers sinking calmly
into a pond's deepest corners,
the air glad as moss for its moisture,
the sky a great arch
of pearled grey, in me,
as it is in heaven.

Beckoning

Outside her opened door,
Mrs. D. calls five flights down,
through dimly-lit corridors,
across chipped and faded tiles,
yellowed, ripened with age,
stale urban smells, my name
enlivened, floating on her tongue,
her warm Irish brogue echoing
through the stairwell of years,
beckoning me up to her place
for raisin bread I can almost taste,
a cup of sweet black tea,
a game of gin rummy,
as she teaches me once again
to shuffle and deal
in timelessness.

Family

The garbage man is Santa.
The nice lady who bends down to say hello,

to ask her name, is my wife, Clara.
She confirms, *That was Clara,*

then points to others we pass
as we walk—the bearded man

is *Uncle Billy*, the rosy-cheeked woman,
Aunt Nina. When I leave,

will she see *Grandma*, too?
All the time, her parents tell me,

and she wonders why
I never stop to say hello.

I wonder if we all might learn
such a global sense of family.

Late August Meditation

Almost my birthday,
a year I nearly didn't complete.
The river's horseshoe bend,
parched by summer's drought,
reflects specks of sun,
as drops of rain—
not enough to sate the fields,
make sparkles of the light.
Stones, once covered by spring rains,
reveal themselves
like glyphs in the shallows,
a message from the past,
whose geology
will outlast our fleeting,
precious, mortal lives.

Arising

I sit in stillness on a snow-covered stone,
a sunny, breezeless day, beneath the bare
and leafless trees, and wait, until my frozen tangle
of a human mind lets go its hold, and matted grasses,
lit by my sudden burning joy for each bowed tree,
shining with its half-melted and refrozen load of snow,
ignite to fill the world with love for all I know
and all I've yet to meet.

III.

Belief

Walking the endless Meseta, we turn to see
yellow broom flowers, orange poppies going by—
the only way to know these pilgrims' progress.

Each night, an ancient town new to us,
steps closer to our journey's end—
we feel no mystic pull toward Santiago,

but we believe in the awe of those who do,
as Gregorian chants pipe through a darkened church,
and a friend we meet weeps freely at a café table.

We leave Castrojeriz in the graying dark,
before dawn, before cafés open, our shoes
tapping a slow rhythm on quiet streets,

and though at this moment they're empty of all but us,
we know the road, the path we've chosen,
takes us somewhere many have gone before.

We feel them all in the hard-packed trail,
in our aching feet,
in our will to keep going, a mysticism we can believe.

Keep Trying

After snowshoeing up the steep hill
in deep swathes of snow, we stop,
beneath a glittering globe of sky
the space of silence opens over us—

standing as if we were the base,
channeling current to a bulb too hot
to touch. We remove gloves, hats,
jackets, in surprising winter heat—

in this quiet spot on the top,
in a forest of would-be lamps, sensing
the thaw that will spark their green,
our lips find each other's.

Gazing upward, stretched out
together on snow, yet apart,
we keep trying, as Mary Oliver,
and the Buddha, instructs,

to make of ourselves a light,
one bright enough to guide us
to kindness, toward ourselves,
toward each other,

toward every living thing—
hoping to carry that shine
back down the hill,
into our separate lives.

Being

She worries about the roofers
who haven't shown up, the excavators
pulling rocks from our yard,
shoring up a sagging foundation,
beans in need of planting,
mulching with straw,
flowers requiring weeding,
bags to pack for our trip.
But it's spring, and I—
hard to admit, but I
need to sit by a stream,
watch sun dazzle water,
flash of red wings over the pond,
sway of new spring grasses.
Like the painted turtle
perched on a log I saw
just yesterday, stunned by the day,
I need to do nothing, but sit,
under the remarkable sun.

Great White

Like *Jaws'*
killer shark

rising from the deep,
cancer cells appear

one morning,
sharp teeth

at her breast,
in the shower.

The First Stage

We bring a taste of home with us,
espresso machine, cream,
my favorite chocolates.
In the common room,
we make friends with our future,
women wearing bright scarves
over baldness, like monks
in some early stage of detachment.

The next day, I push her wheelchair
across an enclosed walkway,
the Bridge of Hope, decorated
with blue and red-painted birds,
Dickinson's *Hope is the Thing
with Feathers* inscribed on the wall.

We rise through each floor
dedicated to a different cancer,
to find our own on the ninth
we try to think of as heaven,
with its summit view of the city
from our infusion suite,
the famous red Citgo triangle of hope
lighting our dark morning,
red brake lights painting the road below,

their reflections and ours
in the windows, blinking
their stop-and-go's,
buses, cars, trucks inching forward,
thin rain turning to snow,
our winter dawn beginning,
as the bright Red Devil—
I'd rather they named
Red Angel, for redemption,
despite its hellish side effects—
inches slowly into Clara's veins.

If this is our Camino,
we're at the first stage,
climbing steep Pyrenees into Spain,
five hundred miles to go,
till we reach the place
of unshakeable faith.

As My Wife Sleeps

Though a brisk, windless day,
two feet of fresh snow,
sky a hard shell of bright azure blue,
the winter sun casts a warm light
along the couch and blanket,
covering her sleeping form,
caressing her left ear
and temple, so aptly named,
as so many pray for her—
friend Awi in Scotland,
Sister Santacitta among the redwoods,
Titia down the street,
Pastor Leon in church,
Clara's mother, aunts,
siblings in Spain,
all wishing her well,
each litany rising through
her body's larger temple,
lighting her sleep like sun
pouring through windows,
transmuting gratitude and faith,
with every calm breath,
as our dogs help too,
napping in a heap
on the living room floor.

Holy Week

A quiet time,
the darkest evening of the year.

We've wrangled a tree
into its bright stand

and wrapped it
in white lights,

our gestures
toward a tentative joy.

A time of pausing,
drawing inward—

dormancy of winter roots.
If only the malignancy, too,

would take this week, at least,
to rest.

Corona Spring

She awaits her next cancer treatment
but the city hospital
reeks of corona contagion.

As we wait for thaw, for rain,
for mitigation, wouldn't you know it—
it snows again.

The Red

The red of the port
scar near her heart

of the Citgo sign's glow
when I turn to the window

of my eyes from watching her
in the infusion bed

the red of the syringe
the nurse inserts into her veins

the red savior drug
to kill all malignancy

the Red Devil
cocktail to save her life

the red I never would have chosen
as the color of hope

the red I now see everywhere
as a sign to believe

Ministrations

I've given up delivering
Meals on Wheels, sitting vigil
for patients in hospice,
offering a chaplain's
bedside attention
to strangers. I focus now
on my wife: pale face,
bald head, a scrub
of hedgehog hair coming in,
so exhausted
by cancer-killing drugs,
she often naps whole afternoons
on the living room couch.
When she notices me
pacing like a caged cat
on behalf of us, our families,
the world in the midst
of pandemic—
then she comes to my side,
patting my arm, cooing,
in comforting tones,
as a mother might,
there, there.

In and Out

My sister limits her horizon
to an assisted living facility,
taken care of in ways she missed
in childhood, and decades
of life afterward.

Quarantined now to one room
by the rampant pandemic,
she's at peace,
enough to let the answering machine
take my call, when I ring
during her stretching routine,
on a towel by her bed.

Snowshoeing with dogs
on a hilltop, having traversed
wet snow, heavy and resistant
as sand, I peel sweaty hat,
gloves and jacket, to cool bare skin
amid forty visible miles,
blue mountains on every side,
no house in sight,
only trees calling to me.

As I focus on a microcosm
of the wide boreal forest--
she finds macrocosm,
in her curtained room.

The Trap Door

Love is a hollowness in the chest,
like feeling each of a tick's eight feet
scurrying through my neck's downy nape,
seeking the perfect site to suck life from me.

Love is an ever-fixed mark, says Will.
He meant steadiness,
but I can't helping thinking *target*.
Love is known from its absence, say I,

when the trap door of loneliness opens
and I fall in—but also by the small glee
of freedom when she's away—
and by our front door's welcome squeaking,
when one of us comes home from roaming.

The Change

We return to the store
where once we imagined
making love in the aisles
between the mangos, kiwis,
and pineapples.
We barely dare a smile,
though I hold her with a look,
as we load a case
of famotidine, tubs
of hand sanitizer,
and sterilized water,
our kisses held back
like green buds
or promises to come—
she doesn't want
to pass the chemo drugs on to me,
I don't want
to give her a cold,
and so we go, morphed
from giggling honeymooners
into seasoned wives
who lean on each other,
strolling along corridors,
choosing sweet ripe kiwis,
cheese from Spain, for treats,
pushing a heavy shopping cart—
having carefully
wiped the handles clean.

Communion

Even if it's still morning,
munch on a few squares
of rich chocolate.
Each chew into lusciousness
will absorb into your being
a sacred wafer of sweet taste
Mayans reserved for worship.
When doctors don't call,
or their diagnoses differ,
when your wife has a seizure
on the operating table—
cocoa wakes you
from the recurring nightmare
with its thick deliciousness,
companioned by a sip of latte,
graceful frothed cream
in the shape of a heart,
held a moment,
dissolving on the tongue,
then swallowed,
with reverence
for the sweetness
gratitude brings.

In the Third Month of Quarantine

For she of the lively brown eyes,
a person in the flesh,
with only six feet between us—
has taken my package
and placed it on the scale,
as a nurse might soothe
a fevered patient—
for she has pressed on stamps
gently as a bandage, as we banter
about the weather, laughing
when I can't name the day—
for she tries with her eyes
to broadcast the smile
hidden by a blue hospital mask,
mine, by flowered cloth—
tempting me to breach, with a hug,
the clear plastic shield
they've strung up
at the post office window
to keep us from just
such pandemic madness.

The Scrims Between Us

Disposable masks and gloves,
six recommended feet
of anxious space from others—

awkward nods to friends we pass
toting groceries in depleted stores—
a wartime feeling I hadn't known before.

In the hospital, corridors strangely quiet,
no visitors allowed, they let me in
to glimpse my wife in the cancer wing.

A scrim of pestilence made visible
by absence spreads around the globe,
a veil between the rest of humanity

and me, where I sit watching
an ash leaf curl in the wind,
wondering how long

it will stay aloft,
how long before it falls, dissolves
and merges with earth.

IV.

From a Far-Off World

As I watch my daughter dance and sing
on the video screen, I can only join virtually,
as a ghost might shadow the living.

Someone bangs a drum I hear in my bones,
strummed by her bright voice,
distinct from the others as my face is to me.

She and her fellow farmers plant and tend
their cooperative Eden, as lambs and calves
get born, sheep shorn, cows milked—

and I feel strangely drained, gazing
from a far-off world, see her as I imagine
she'll be when I'm gone.

I visit my sons, their wives and little ones,
though we cannot breathe on each other,
or touch, my rectangle floating above theirs

like a Cubist idea of family, as we peer
at each other through a glass, blurred.
I see them living more wholly

than I would dare to ask,
and happiness shapes my face—
so to what do I owe this knife in my gut?

Color Coding

When I see onscreen,
on the evening news,
how the officer of peace
presses his knee
into George Floyd's neck
on the street,
until he no longer pleads
or breathes—I don't think
of the cop stopping me
for speeding on our rural road,
offering this middle-aged granny
a warning, and a compliment
for my dog to put me at ease—
I don't think until after my keening.

Two Halves

I sit in the sun in May
by a flat of strawberry plants
I plan to hoe into thick mulch
and loam as she directs:

Four in the garden's heart,
three against the edges,
dig in deep, water just enough
to nourish the roots.

Fine as baby or angel hair,
their secondary filaments delicate
as breath, I'll gentle the roots into rich soil
Clara's worked for decades,

as she nurses her post-surgical chest,
arms too swollen to use.
I limp from a leg injury,
after months of walking too much,

six hundred miles since January,
hiking daily over steep hills,
to ease the strain of caretaking,
until my legs gave out.

I plant from a chair, as she, the gardener,
stands, hands at her sides,
we two halves hoping for a whole harvest
sometime this summer.

Sledding the Valley of the Shadow

We're burning the Earth. We're burning the sky.
—Deena Metzger

I know the burning's true,
so I won't be throwing snowballs
in the halls of Congress.

After today's snowfall, I grab jacket, hat, mittens,
tear down the steep drive on my orange sled,
beaming a path through the night with a light

I hold between my knees
under the spread of winter constellations,
as dogs lope alongside.

In this northern woods valley,
we're more likely to hear geese
than airplanes overhead.

I sled and snowshoe through cold winter days
I believe will last through my lifetime,
but still act for the generations after.

I compost, recycle, keep bees,
have forgone meat for thirty years, and wonder how else to please,
whether being the change I'd like to see

will be enough to ease the anxiety
spreading like wildfire from teen to teen, every Greta or Deena
grieving the oblivion yet to come.

Our First Wedded Death

He'd rouse us every morning,
face resting on the edge
of the bed, long black nose,
mingling his breath with ours.
When the vet arrives with her syringe,
a blue potion to end the pain
of tumors and arthritic spine,
we sit with him until our friend
is gone, his body still, on the lawn.
The other dogs look on,
then away, as if the loss
were beyond comfort.

The Croissant

My wife has baked croissants
as a Sunday treat,
in this odd time of quarantine,
days made tasteless by isolation,
and the jam is raspberry,
gleaming redly at me in morning sun.
One buttery, flaky moment
on the tongue returns me
to twenty-three,
to the Hungarian café on Amsterdam,
tucked into the blanketing shadow
of St. John the Divine.
The jam I taste today
is not tart raspberry,
but the honeyed apricot
the café served then,
as Clara and I watch
church on a phone
propped against a book,
as the pastor, our friend,
intones kind words
for the loss of our shepherd Alys,
while a candle he lit for her
flickers in the empty church
that gently echoes his words,
as the last bite crackles
against my palate
and melts in the nave
of mouth—this bit of now.
We struggle all day to stay
in place, as some instinct
teases us to stray—illusory
as memory's preserves—

till this flaky bite
of just here, just now,
this crispy crumb
of all that's left,
butters the tongue.

On the Eve of June

May's last day
seems time enough
to speak of time's passing,
knowing she'll see,
suddenly on her calendar,
a few dreaming hours from now,
a whole new month opened up.
After we read a storybook
together by video,
I show her Chloe,
asleep on the rug at my feet,
then say of our other dog,
Alys, *She was old,*
and, last week, she died.
I add comfort for her—or me,
Now she's... somewhere,
flying in the clouds.
I stare out at the rose bush
where we planted her ashes,
soil still disturbed,
bush not yet rooted.
I pull a long face,
so she will understand
this is *a sad event,*
but she breaks in,
in her bright, clear voice:
No Grandma,
Alys has just gone home—
her old one.
Then I sing Raffi's
Willoughby Wallaby Woo,
and she dances circles
unbroken by grief.

Inversions

Suddenly on my back,
legs aloft like a stranded beetle
or yoga pose gone wrong—
I lie, thinking of Kafka,
waiting as my wife exclaims,
This isn't normal!
and I can still hear
on my open computer
the Zoom poetry group
I'm supposed to be hosting,
chatting about fonts
and poem spacing,
as they wait for me
to return to the meeting,
unable to hear my moans.
Due soon at the hospital
for oncology, Clara,
bald and weak,
has to hobble me to the car,
then into a wheelchair
we scrounge
from the lobby,
she out of breath,
pushing me,
her doctor marveling
at the pair of us
as we all chuckle—
me, clutching my inflamed calf,
he, wondering
which of us to treat.

To Santiago

We began climbing in the year's darkest days,
diagnosis in late November, turning trips
to the cancer center's mountain into adventure.

Tying a scallop shell to her hospital backpack,
we metaphored illness as a pilgrimage to Santiago,
eight chemo treatments, followed by surgery.

We trekked December's steep bitter peaks,
January's icy valleys. *How many miles*, we'd say,
about halfway, sometime in snowy February.

We slogged on through a wet March,
a windy April that didn't seem like spring.
Though our feet didn't develop blisters,

her heart raced at an alarming rate,
she lost her hair, and her taste buds changed.
A bit metallic, she'd say, with grit.

As we approached surgery, in early May,
we searched the horizon for the cathedral,
knew the steeple would soon come into view.

Soon we'd descend the final hill to Santiago.
Soon the maroon-robed priests
would swing the *Botafumeiro* over our heads,

fill the vast space with cleansing fragrance
of myrrh and frankincense. Soon we'd stroll
along the beach at the end of the world,

the beach that ends one world
and begins another, and cancer
would become a wintry memory.

That Splendid Thing

After I lose the tomatoes and basil to frost,
hoe under bean plants, peppers, squash and melons,
late blooming strawberries exhausted with fruit,
after the daily calamities announced on the news—
shutdowns in Paris, Tokyo, Rio, New York,
anxieties of injustice, unfair elections—
amass and cover my heart and my mind,
I have to sit for a long while away from other humans,
my only companions a soft autumn wind,
a canine friend, oaks trembling with rust,
maples about to blaze into flame, and a striped,
hairy caterpillar crawling over my leg,
its long silver hairs shining in the temporary sun,
reminding me I'm here now,
I'm alive, that still splendid thing.

The Most Important Thing,
I Learn from My Granddaughter

After her long drive home
over mountains to the sea,

her dad films her, sends it to me—
pushing the toy shopping cart I gave her,

with only a diaper for clothes,
she announces to dolls, to corridor walls,

I'm here!
I'm here!
I'm here!

A presence I hear ringing so loudly here,
among towering hemlocks, I look to see

who's speaking—not the crow overhead,
nor snow, hills, nor limb breaking in wind,

this ringing I hear buying groceries
from a masked cashier, as I pass friends

entering as I exit, all of us hurrying
to somewhere else, the ringing I hear

looking into my wife's eyes as I serve
her coffee—I realize the one singing

I'm here!
I'm here!
I'm here!

is me.

Harvest

After months of quarantine,
I leave our hill,

drive through valley fog, over mountains
through dissipating mist to sunlit beach,

visit once again my kin,
carrying the sweetness I've crushed

from wax, filtered, sieved
but not heated, a raw deep goodness,

gift from spring's maple flowers,
summer's clover, autumn's goldenrod,

all the seasons I've missed them,
alchemized to this jar of liquid gold.

Joy and Sorrow

Both emotions weigh about the same, but one
opens you up, like a cavity, a deep well
you think will never fill, the liquid loss
of a friend's voice, the way she turned a phrase.

The other's helium—walking on the same agèd feet,
but hardly noticing soles on cold pavement,
light as a leaf riding a breeze.
When you hold your grandson for the first time,

in his little star suit, his two pools of deep blue
beam into you; his long fingers curl and uncurl,
like lilies at dawn or dusk, air you still breathe,
as you hover that night like a balloon over your bed,

still hearing your friend's waterfall notes,
finally knowing both joy and sorrow are holy.

In Town, after Quarantine

Newly in my body
in morning's gentle warmth,
a thin tee all I need
between me and the weather,
outside my favorite café,
with a frothed cortado,
burrito with salsa,
black beans, sour cream—
every scent rising,
mask dangling at my neck
like a crab's castoff shell,
breathing in the June-soft air,
raucous sounds of a passing truck,
so welcome after months
alone together at home—
at home among strangers,
men women children I do not know,
except in my bones, studying
glad faces from a distant table,
the chatting fragments I overhear,
clear waters eddying stones,
more sating than the burrito
and cortado—the magnificent
rusted cars passing, the clean,
shiny cars passing—all swimming
like trout in a river, frolicking
beneath the wide, rippled-blue sky.

Through the Bardo

She shall go to the bardo
again one day,

as she did before,
but less encumbered.

She left a kitchen, newly reincarnated,
a roof re-tinned in forest green.

She left three hayfields
she knew every fecund inch of,

gloves worn to ghosts
of their former selves.

The bardo looked like a road,
then a churning river, wide as Lethe,

a sojourn prone to mists and fogs
and sun-dazzled water.

She returned to her old body
with a re-birthed ego,

as joys and griefs sieved through her
like juice from fruit.

She shall go again one day.
You see, she knows the way.

The Ineffable

Through the window, I could see,
amid spring's new green,
in the way my wife bent to the puppy,
the way they tugged on a toy,
her pleasure in her healed frame,
hair restored to its thick mane,
her life feeling just right.
Back in the house, she practices vibrato,
her deep alto rising through the floorboards,
the roof on the house rising too,
the sky opening, for both of us.

I Stopped

and turned, to see,
on my periphery,
what played such a gentle note—
cresting the field's edge,
full of rustling yellow leaves,
a line of twenty or thirty
slender poplar trees,
the midday sun singling out
each leaf equally.

I turned, saw and listened,
knowing that all was good—
if today proved to be my last on Earth,
I would be grateful I had stopped
to see the dancing poplar trees,
all those jeweled bits of light.

All of It

Remember the fluctuating sea,
morning on the beach, the sun's
orange disk, like a porthole into divine fire.
Remember the seals, one then another,
bobbing up, as if to play, or say hello.
Remember the swim, the sharp rock,
the gash on your leg, remember
the bee sting reddening your ear,
the itch and swelling, with something
to tell the wandering mind.
Remember the hard walk, the cobblestones,
the steps on the path, remember
the church services, the vespers,
the nuns blessing your knee.
Remember the time—not long ago—
a day closed you into an ambulance,
your heart beating too fast to bear, remember
being lifted up in the air, waving goodbye,
calling out: *Tell the children, please.*
Remember the peace in returning to dogs,
to house, to your wife Clara lit within,
remember swimming in the pond again,
in a body made new by gratitude.

Notes

We Are Ready

"We Are Ready" is my response to Justice Brett Kavanaugh's 2018 confirmation hearing, featuring Christine Blasey Ford's scathing testimony

Offstage

Lines from Shakespeare's *The Winter's Tale*

On Earth

Lines from The Lord's Prayer, King James Version

Belief

In 2018 my wife Clara Giménez and I walked the Camino, a 500 mile pilgrimage across northern Spain, ending at the Cathedral of Santiago

Keep Trying

"Make of yourself a light" is from Mary Oliver's "The Buddha's Last Instruction"

The First Stage

"Hope is the Thing With Feathers," a line from Emily Dickinson, is painted on the Bridge of Hope, connecting Boston's Brigham and Women's Hospital with the Dana Farber Cancer Institute

Red Devil is a chemotherapy drug, named for its distinctive red color

The Trap Door
Lines from Shakespeare's sonnet 116

Sledding the Valley of the Shadow
Greta refers to the young Swedish environmental activist, Greta Thunberg

Deena Metzger is an American writer, healer and activist

The Croissant
Rev. Dr. Leon Dunkley is the Pastor of North Chapel Unitarian Universalist Church in Woodstock, Vermont

To Santiago
The Botafumeiro is a famous thurible used at the Cathedral of Santiago to create a cleansing aroma of incense to sweeten the air over flocks of tired pilgrims

Acknowledgments

Grateful acknowledgment is made to the editors of the journals and anthologies who first published the following poems. The poems, sometimes in earlier versions, appeared as follows:

Alaska Quarterly: "The Something"
Atlanta Review: "Intimations of Adulthood"
Buddhist Poetry Review: "I Stopped," "The Most Important Thing, I Learn from my Granddaughter"
Crosswinds Poetry Journal: "Joy and Sorrow," "That Splendid Thing"
Drunk Monkeys: "The Frother Whisk"
Everything We Need, Headmistress Press: "The First Stage," "To Santiago," "Madre"
Gathering Project: "From a Far-Off World"
Gemini Poetry Prize, Honorable Mention: "Madre"
Grateful Living: "The Once Invisible Garden"
Joe Gouveia Outermost Poetry Contest, Honorable Mention: "Letter to Sally"
Journal of the American Medical Association: "Bumpy Country"
Lavender Review: "All of It"
Limerick Arts Stony Thursday Poetry Book: "The Change"
Live Encounters: "Coastal Globe," "In the Village Store"

Lois Cranston Poetry Prize Runner Up, Calyx Press: "Not a
Metaphor"

Muddy River Poetry Review: "Belief"

The Museum of Americana: "East of Eden," "Two Halves"

Northern Woodlands: "Our Own Orion"

One Art: "Someone"

One Jacar Press: "The Weight of Him (Postmortem Parenting
part two)"

Pangyrus: "The Red"

PB Magazine: The Covid Diaries, Ireland: "The Scrims Between
Us"

Peregrine Journal: "Conjuration"

Poets Reading the News: "We Are Ready"

The Quaranzine: Poetry in the Time of COVID-19: "The Croissant"

Quartet Journal: "The River"

Quill and Parchment: "Being," "Ministrations," "The Trap
Door"

Red Eft Review: "Keep Trying"

River Styx: "In the Dental Chair (Postmortem Parenting part
one)"

Sheila-Na-Gig: "The Once Invisible Garden"

Silver Birch Press: "Sledding the Valley of the Shadow"

Spiritus, Johns Hopkins University Press: "On Earth"

Thanks

With much gratitude to the poetry fellowship of the Wednesday Poets: Peg Brightman, Lynne Byler, Jon Escher, Deb Franzoni, Brooke Herter James, Jill Herrick Lee, Sarah Snyder; to the River Poets: Sue Burton, Pam Harrison (in memory), Anne Shivas, Clyde Watson, Carol Westberg. Thank you to poetry workshop leaders Ellen Bass, Marie Howe, Rick Barot, Kim Addonizio, for your generosity, patience, dedication and skill. Thank you to April Ossmann for untiring and always spot-on editorial advice. Thank you to Eric Muhr and Fernwood Press for bringing *Sledding the Valley of the Shadow* into beautiful form. Thank you to our choir director Diane Mellinger for giving me the task of providing one video poem a week for our North Chapel Sunday Service, all through COVID (over sixty recordings), helping me to feel heard. Thank you Clara for being the first reader for most of these poems, for offering helpful feedback, and for recovering so beautifully from such a challenging illness, all while COVID kept us isolated on our hill. Thank you to the gods for providing the occasional snowstorm, and with gratitude to our steep, curved driveway, a perfect length for sledding.

About the Author

Laura Foley is the author of seven full-length poetry collections and three chapbooks. *Why I Never Finished My Dissertation* received a starred Kirkus Review, an Eric Hoffer Award, and was longlisted for the Julie Suk Award from Jacar Press. She has won a Narrative Magazine Poetry Prize, The Common Good Books Poetry Prize, the Bisexual Book Award, Atlanta Review's Grand Prize and others. Her work has been included in many journals and anthologies, including *Alaska Quarterly*, *Valparaiso Poetry Review*, *DMQ Review*, JAMA, Poetry Society London, *Atlanta Review*, *Poetry of Presence*, *The Wonder of Small Things*, and *How to Love the World*. Her poems have been featured frequently on *The Writer's Almanac*. She lives with her wife, Clara Giménez, and their two romping canines on the steep banks of the Connecticut River in New Hampshire.

Title Index

First Line Index